ANCESTRAL DEMON OF A GRIEVING BRIDE

MARY BURRITT CHRISTIANSEN
POETRY SERIES · *Hilda Raz, Series Editor*

The Mary Burritt Christiansen Poetry Series publishes two to four books a year that engage and give voice to the realities of living, working, and experiencing the West and the Border as places and as metaphors. The purpose of the series is to expand access to, and the audience for, quality poetry, both single volumes and anthologies, that can be used for general reading as well as in classrooms.

Also available in the Mary Burritt Christiansen Poetry Series:

The Definition of Empty: Poems by Bill O'Neill
Feel Puma: Poems by Ray Gonzalez
Grief Land: Poems by Carrie Shipers
The Shadowgraph: Poems by James Cihlar
Crosscut: Poems by Sean Prentiss
The Music of Her Rivers: Poems by Renny Golden
to cleave: poems by Barbara Rockman
After Party: Poems by Noah Blaustein
The News as Usual: Poems by Jon Kelly Yenser
Gather the Night: Poems by Katherine DiBella Seluja

For additional titles in the Mary Burritt Christiansen Poetry Series, please visit unmpress.com.

ANCESTRAL DEMON
of a GRIEVING BRIDE

••••

SY HOAHWAH *poems*

UNIVERSITY OF NEW MEXICO PRESS ✦ ALBUQUERQUE

ISBN 978-0-8263-6221-6 (paper)

ISBN 978-0-8263-6222-3 (electronic)

Library of Congress Cataloging-in-Publication data
is on file with the Library of Congress.

COVER ILLUSTRATION *skull* pauljuser | istockphoto.com

paper textures from the designer's collection

DESIGNED BY Mindy Basinger Hill

COMPOSED IN Adobe Jenson Pro and Sabler Titling

FOR ISIS, PHOENIX, AND SONNY

who made me see that fine line

between me and Time

CONTENTS

ANCESTRAL DEMON OF A GRIEVING BRIDE

HILLBILLY LEVIATHAN

The Ozarks are where defeated assassins, the unholy,
and monsters come to retire.
Proper soil and crooked moonlight grow back
the disemboweled, the decapitated
while we collect arrears in child support for our demigod children.

Procession of taillights lined deep down the logging trails.
Along the way, there was a gentleman arguing with his soul
over his suicide.

I, tongue of snakes,
cut up, dipped in powdered sugar,
scattered to the ants in the deepest corner of Mt. Nebo.
The insult binds my ghost to the mountain.

Typhoon collected the few precious scales left of me
from the undertow.
My southern accent-muscle burned up
from haunting your life/house.

Now, let daybreak be my head and the year my whole body.
An online southern Christian university ordained my smoker's cough
to be a dove.

My favorite exorcism:
The demon, steeped in cornbread philosophy,
who does not have enough ass to carry off the jeans he advertises
as he kneels down to the priest and holy water.

Years ago, as a child, I climbed the levee and made a hole in the air.
That's where I will rest, but the gate is not wide enough.
Like my burial site, I am party size.

BIOGRAPHY

This is more valuable as my talisman than as my biography.
As a child, father told me I hatched out of a pearl partially dissolved in wine.

Mother always reminded me, I reminded her of father,
and I made the milk curdle in the stomach of other newborns.

A high ceiling was our family's dining table,
where light was easy to swallow.

Father had a low-wage body and pushed around a coffin
full of Kahlua and coke.

Daily, mother read my father's obituary aloud
in a tone between poetry and a backward prayer.

Our first winter living in town, my brother became touched
after he sipped accumulated frost off a mausoleum.

I remember the weave of sunlight etched across his face.
Me, my whole life, determined to read the Devil's mind,
to reach in, pull out the brain, open to a random page,
read about my future from the bottom to top.

TOWARD MT. SCOTT

Toward Mt. Scott
it is sharp as a knife.

The bad roads lead to lost roads.
The lost roads lead to the same empty spot.

People sometimes go
to lonely places for power.

Eagles sometimes are choked,
dragonflies lassoed.

Smaller birds follow ghosts
to eat off the bugs.

Line of barbed wire
marks the boundary
between this world
and the next.

3

NOTED TO BE THE DEFINITIVE
BRIGHT MORNING
OF TEN THOUSAND CALENDARS

Noted to be the definitive bright morning of ten thousand calendars,

the church bell melted.
Rage of unrequited love became a terrible serpent.

The morning star lowered like an enemy's flag.
A vampire's mattress tumbled out at the outskirts of town.

Ancient lanterns, suddenly thrown through the air,
somewhere deep in the mountains.

That night, in a snowy rural area, an elderly, powder-faced woman
appeared on doorsteps in search of wine.

Her origins, neatly wrapped in the cold dressing of a snowflake's breath.

PINEOLA

Severed finger of a convicted murderer uncurls like a waking pet.
Demonic compass points toward the most dangerous direction to get home.

Its long, yellow fingernail can pick any lock.

On the fishhook, the finger resembles a long, fat mealworm.
Most times it's lodged in the throats of my enemies
or hiding among the tampons of cops' wives.

It avoids gold rings; it's bad luck.

When wearing this rot relic on a chain,   5
sunlight smells like stale curtains in a worn-out hearse.
Rain never hits my clothes.

Rooms seem hotter.
Radios turn on by themselves, always to the same Lucinda Williams song.
Use any mirror as a doorway, I come out into the same sweaty
bedroom from a previous life.

I forget who is wearing whom.

I pierce the fingertip to draw up a will.
I dip it in water. I point it toward the sun. I flick it to make rain.

Hanging on the wall,
I sleep under this bird, booger-picker, dream catcher,
missing piece of an inverted crucifix, rotting pencil.

It sleeps over me like an accusative God.

Around midnight I wake up. The finger is typing in the next room.
What is it composing at this time of night?

Letters to a parole board,
love letters to the rest of the hand,
midnight sermons,
ransom notes pertaining to me,
memoirs about life, hanging from my neck . . .

EVER SINCE I CAN REMEMBER

Ever since I can remember,
the decapitated head sings

about being
in a brass bucket

at the foot of a cold mountain.
Then it chases us.

Lightning
tied to its hair,

jagged teeth glow.
Voice sharpened

on the stones
swallowed.

Speed up
slow down

a vengeance
old tribal times.

COUNTY LINE

9:13 a.m. Saline County.
The sun slowly crosses the hair
in the eyepiece of the dead mother coming down,
looking around for her children.

Horses expand
and empty out into a field
singed in the grease of strength.
Sunlight keeps its hugs to a minimum.

A hornet drifts into a deserted house around
the waist of silence. Underneath the porch,
butterfly wings melt in cat saliva.

I am shy
and have the reputation of a basement corner.

I can hear the circulatory system
of a spider nesting in my ears.

The spider cross-stitches its silk with my veins,
creating the center of a second sky.

My name has reached the hilltops
but is forgotten in the morning light.

IT'S BEEN 145 YEARS;
I AM STILL SURRENDERING
TO FT. SILL

after Charles Simic

It's been 145 years; I am still surrendering to Ft. Sill.
The Quohada went one way, the Kiowa another.
The Cheyenne even another way.
We're all cutting off fingertips, leaving trails of direction.
The moon is the body and the funeral.
Thistle is tall enough to be silence.
We've all been chased to this genocidal beauty once or twice,
surrendering at a fast-food table with free Wi-Fi.
The stench of the run on our beaded kicks.
We're unable to tell the difference
between the glow of smart maps
and campfires of all who are closing in
with ATM cards and 4G in hand.
Even the dead land surveyor from Subiaco is right.
There is no sanctuary in the subdivisions we edge closer to
with our bowstrings cut.

GLITTER

My sinister-bent laugh descends
into its own smirk of fire,

and the smoke follows the most beautiful.

The Great Magnet points
the iron in my blood toward the woods.

I dry-fit moonlight to the openings
of my fox skull. It is a church of hunger.

10   The hunted unfold the wilderness
from their hearts.

I follow . . .
These are walking-alone stars.

Their glitter I devour
when these apostle-bodies are charged with the word.

The rest, a mouthful of feathers
spat out over the mountains.

GREASY VOICE

I smell like the roads
cutting through the peanut fields.

My dance steps
sound like the emptiness of barns.

The janitor of hell sweeps up
the coffin nails and bouquets of dead horseflies
after me.

I'm a dazed underworld hero fleshed and rubbed down
with my own tongue and brains.

The grease of me bubbling like an enchanted lake.

I don't even have ashes of dead saints
to rub into my eyes.

Mud-clown face
with laughter and grease spraying out,
following the hairy tail of a balding star.

I carry the power lines of hell around my neck.
My only wing hangs on an empty wall.

HINTERLANDS

My ancestors were not diligent,
and so they lived beside the fort
that's neither on the maps of heaven
nor of hell.
In these lands, there is no difference
between a star and thrown car keys.
Chicken nuggets hatch from the eggs of eagles.
I grow dirty while bathing in bottled water.
My bed comforter is a wet parking lot
I wrap myself up in.
If I eat in the morning, there's nothing left in the evening.
My dish of grass and cigarette butts is topped with expired coupons.
Stir all I like, I never swallow it down.
All the while, my rabbit's foot runs about
from Las Cruces to West Memphis,
searching for flawless luck.
The more one cries, the more one prospers . . .
O ancestral demon, may my lamentation become verbal sorcery.

IN THE MONTH
OF CLEANING FAMILY PLOTS

In the month of cleaning family plots, I learned football among graves.
All summer, fangs were plentiful. I fed only on fruit and acorns next
    to a nest
built in a discarded doll's head that marked the fifty-yard line.
From snakes licking my ears, sounds of trees, and whispers from
    the dead
I learned to read plays by how the opposing team huddled.
On the field I gave the appearance of lightning, a wardrobe of
    open wounds.
Magical goon who knew a love that outlasted bottles of tequila and
    all the Cure albums.
It, too, was true.

TUHUVITU

Out of hunger,
the abyss cooks itself in boiling water,
meat loosens from its bones.

By looking through a clear plastic spoon,
I count the outlines of scorpions and upside-down goddesses
caught in the fibers of the Milky Way's gristle.

Searching for the rat tail–handled tool of his trade,
an occultist feels the texture of obsidian floors
leading to the roaring tomb of a forgotten silent-movie star.

Black-hooded cloak,
black bandages
unravel to the black teeth
of a bony lady reciting the abysmal alphabet
of a flower that's dark as possible.

For decades, tubercular-child sounds
echo from a walled-up entrance of an ancient turret
where heathen constellations tore their underbellies upon.

The grieving bride hides the moonlight from the moon
in every hem of her deceased's dress suit.

Á CONQUES

Stained glass reflects the sky,
full of an aging god's hair that's falling out.

Silver embankments upon silver embankments
mentioned only in folklore.

Like cut-up bedsheets and used bandages
of dead saints and martyrs,
a hundred windows heal the daylight.

I press the sunset's Luciferian face against the glass,
jimmy a window to crawl in and save myself
in the last minute of light.

NON-NATIVE VERSION

I'm always the skeleton;
you, soul, the trash bag.

It never mentions you
melting away

in the noisy stomachs
of scavengers,

or how the moonlight feels around in tall weeds
for spent shells,

why the dumpsite is nicknamed
"The Playground,"

nor why my sleep is a long tunnel.
I always wake up,
my skin and clothes come rushing to me.

Death kneeling at the entrance,
cleaning his nails with a pocketknife.

For that entrance,
I traced your skeleton onto butcher paper.

I couldn't help but think
how empty your skeleton looked,

like an exotic zoo before a storm,
Death says.

KJV

I only remember the bible,
not the man, my grandfather.
When he read from it, the bible sounded
bird-broken as it was slammed down,
scaring away the ghosts licking the filth
from the corners of our kitchen.

Grandfather buried with his favorite bible—
thick brochure on heaven and hell
expected to be read in the dark
of the casket
as the pounds of dirt settle softly like sleep.
The rainwater prying open
the hieroglyphics of my grandfather's bones.
His soul, a label with directions
on how to clean with the heat
of a cold-spoken, biblical word.

And his bible is, at least, a century old by now.
It will have grown legs
to kick in the darkness.

A mouth to eat through the upholstery and dirt as it digs free,
a long, protruding tongue to flick at the moon.
The bible will scurry away like a tarantula before the first rain.
It will realize its own hot war and cold god.
It will both curse and pray.

KUNG-FU OF BEING SILENT

It wasn't a hole, it was a howl
filled with pine needles,

baby possum skulls,
and homecoming.

Pine trees stood in twos like pallbearers.
The bark read like scripture.

Sunlight tore off into self-serving size.

The day's entry written
on the rising smoke of a long procession,

driverless hearses
and real wolves.

Upwind, a tomb of antlers
asked my shadow for its hide

to lay a needle on its groove,
to hear its music.

BEGET

Out in the dark,
my father's house is telling itself stories
about my father going back to his birthplace,
how his skull was the color of a meteor.

My father's birthplace gives fellowships to lightning
and defense contracts to tornadoes.
When there is no one to pursue,
the sunlight gets fat on apples and wedding toasts.

There are the stories about my father's ex-wives:
a mountain
and a river.

When he divorced them:
the mountain slid down onto a small farming community.
The drowned were left huddled in the corner
when the river flowed in reverse to follow him.

When my father finally left his house, the trees gutted a storm.
Doves spilled out from its breastbone.

LOGGING-TRAIL ANGEL

That day my guardian angel was cast out,
she responded, *"Fine, your heaven is too bougie,
and your hell is too plain!"*

Then she packed up her one washcloth, one bath towel,
and my best button-up shirt.

Ever since, we tried every doorknob and followed every mouse trail
to get out of this promised land.

We've been living
out of the potholes of back roads.

Along a logging trail, a crow attacked her washcloth.
It looked like an owl when it got wet.

The towel wore down to a warm breath on my skin.
When I dried off it melted away in the last rain.

My button-up shirt, it has been so long,
I think was a product of my imagination.

But I can finally hear the trumpet in the East that others talk about.
Sunlight never catches up to us.
We can board with the shadows
and not on pine needles gathered on the steeple.

It's neck to neck:
Shadow vs. Light
Black Hat vs. White Hat
Number 6 vs. Number 7
Snake vs. Dove
Oil vs. Water
Fork vs. Spoon

We are even back to trying doorknobs.
At midnight, do you hear us knocking three times?

MOURNERS

The sister breaks the blade, cutting another's hair.
Their brother killed by a jealous husband.
Tonight, a flood of calf births sweeps in from the wildlife refuge.

At the supper table
one with six fingers passes out plastic spoons.
Another sister seasons the corn soup with gunpowder.
Rolling up a pack of cigarettes in a short sleeve of moonlight,
doctoring myself until I hear a stray bark.
Dead brother hums a '49 song.

Next morning,
sunken reddish muddy sun
climbs on clay, bone, stone, and fresh obituaries.
One mourner wades out in the middle of starlings, Rumchata,
    and coffee.
The other uses grasshopper legs
to pick the family locker box at Lake Bottom.
The dead brother gives voice inside the throat of a stray.

For the locker box, one mourner writes down family genealogy.
The other writes about the ancestral demon.
Dead brother hides from the others
and burns their manuscripts, one by one.

I become the patron saint of empty tables.
After the funeral
everything is dozing, abandoned.

The only sound, the younger sister
walking off to drink with a stranger
where snakes and honeysuckle intertwine.

NATIVE CHILD STAR

In that movie about the plains,
I was an extra.
That's me there, I told the grandkids,
in a scene of tall grass
squeezed between sunlight and blood.

Hours upon hours in this historical makeup.
Actors on their war ponies tripping over fish line.
Special lighting made actresses appear inside out.
Womanhood spread out like a battlefield map.
Shocked, I couldn't tell the difference
between prop babies and cannonballs.

Take, after take, after take,
they rewound the bullets. We ran,
with sabers grazing our hair,
until the cavalry horses stood dazed
in the wide-open mouth of night.
The village was long gone,
but the director gestured to his cameramen
to keep rolling.

SIX FINGERS

They say the snake is the severed tail
of a vast and dangerous creature of filth and fog.
I can relate to that.
I am the cutoff,
the stump.
My life, at best, is a severed hand with six fingers.
A skinny cardinal for a wedding ring.
My blood trail disappears up
up into the trees,
into the sky,
into the next world.
Starry hand of dawn,
all six fingers pointing in six different directions,
fingering goodbye.
Undecided, I sat here long enough
to become an altar
where the abandoned monsters come to pray.
My temple of one hundred wildernesses,
shiny like the edges of a viper's eye.
The offerings—dead spiders, hummingbirds,
and crispy, sun-soaked leaves raked out of cemetery lawns.

SKIN PETALS

These are the fragile petals from the last Spaniards' shirts
before the gold drove them mad.
Mother had stripped their blood-orange sun
from their heads
and sprinkled blooms over their skulls.
She took the bloom from their roses
and fists,
carefully pulled each one apart
until they covered our table.
She squeezed them. We rubbed the extract
into the folds of our turquoise skin.
Plucks of skin petals
floated in cold water
while their bones mixed
with the sugar and flour of heaven,
forever stranded in the dough of a hundred-handed God.

LAST COMANCHE ALLOTMENT
AT THE EDGE OF THE WORLD

Around the dining-room window,
the deceased's hair pressed
inside books.
Portrait of Quanah Parker with Jesus as a water bird.

The farmhouse stands dusk on the hill.
Clouds are slanted.

Sunset slides back down into its blood bucket.
Flies encrypt secrets in the sky.

The bee, inside a cow skull,
tries to construct its own landscape:
god
sky
pine trees

The buzzing to pin this all:
what it believes in
what it hopes for
what it leaves behind.

Half asleep, the bee falls,
convincing the cow skull of eternity.

Barnyard swallows the flies.
The barn: a question.
Hay and fire have sex.

Lips surface to taste the ash.
Horses confused with smoke.

Hogs pack their belongings
into their floppy hats.

They are having one experience
in a darkening field.

I have a green tractor.

TYPHONI

This is the deepest part of the world.

Birds don't fly here,
but there is the sound of wings.

The smell, just a struggle in the earth
underneath the musty floorboards.

Monsters hatch fully grown from their eggs.
Snaky legs indicate chaos.

I carry sad omens,

slobber down the psychic's legs
to her feet pointed backward,

roll off the back of a skull strapped on top
of the fox who shapeshifts into the irresistible.

A Christian, Oklahoma-shaped and melancholic,
caught at the entrance of a ditch
as the best breath of me tornadoes into the next county.

WHAT IS LEFT

What is left
of my family's 160 acres:
a lone pecan tree
on the fringe of Cache Creek.

A squirrel runs up and down the trunk
carrying insults
between my dead grandfather
and the birds living in the top branches.

I carve my name
on the moon's teeth.

CHURCH FOR THE DISLIKED

On the turnpike, the smell of a heaven
made out of old barnwood
from Okmulgee.

Handles and rungs
cut from a fat farmer's leather belt.

In the eastern counties,
coffins raced uphill, rolling on hay bales
and billiard balls.

30 Charon paid for everyone at the I-44 tollbooth.

On the North Canadian,
comforts of a widower's loneliness
floated on pontoons.

Time balanced on a fish egg.

In the city, violins violated jackhammers.
At the refuge, night is the church for the disliked.
I go to baptize the plants, horns, and rain.

I have passed through many different Oklahoma statehoods.

BEFORE WE'RE EATEN

Before we're eaten . . .
the raccoon-witch-cannibal-monk sings to us,
showing rows upon rows of teeth.
The songs are always about the Arapaho girl
whose parents' names are White Crazy and Grief
and how she offers up her last finger as a sacrifice.
Then the cannibal monk takes a bow,
wearing his own gigantic scrotum as a robe.
At the center of the center of the center of things,
he keeps us.
His stomach is a small bedroom
with an old mattress and wooden floor
lined with old newspapers
and coffee cans full of kerosene
for the scorpions that come out to mock.

BLACK HAW

Black silk handkerchief
over a glass of four-day-old rainwater
from the birdbath of a house
where patricide was committed.

It shows me sickness,
the work of a snake-bone hag
who takes up residence in a wood pile
behind the liquor store at the county line.

Tonight is nothing but a cardinal
pursued by the brutal abyss.

Tonight is nothing but an identity
consisting of only two feelings: dim and ruin.

Tonight is nothing but blackened teeth.

I look out of the house.
Snake-bone hag is rising
with the blood-bucket moon,
a water moccasin wrapped around one arm,
a diamondback wrapped around the other.

Before morning light slaps the rooftop
I have to have breakfast done.

I have to eat breakfast with no one walking behind me,
no shadows cast over my plate.

A young woman's death, doubled-spaced.
Her cough smells like pennies.

I suck out a rattler's broken fang
penetrating her heart and back.

To fight off infection, she will have to chew
on black haw and sage.

On my way home, the ghost of the young woman's mother
tries to pay me with a handful of dead leaves.

CRIES BY NIGHT WITH HEAD BELOW,
FEET ABOVE

One summer, a serial killer hid out in our county
in the darkest corner of the darkest mountain,
circled by the darkest deer.

I dreamt about search parties and mountain mist
rubbing up against her bare heels.

She, combing her hair,
caused musical instruments to be heard but not seen.
She wasn't visible in the daylight.

But at night she spread his madness about
through the stars.
Trees swayed at the sound of her voice.

It made those who ran, stand still.
She could retrieve runaways if she wanted.

At night, one saw only her language of pale-red flame
hovering in darkness, shedding no radiance
upon the piney surfaces over which it glided,
generating truth and falsehood,
good and evil,
light and darkness
with the same words.

WHEN SNAKE WAS DOVE'S
BROTHER-IN-LAW

When Snake was Dove's brother-in-law
midnight whistled across the lake.

I drank scotch and survived on pine needles.
For a headache I dug a trench long enough for a body.

The lake turned over like a heartbroken spouse.
An albino largemouth bass surfaced.

All its fins and ancient hooks pointed toward heaven.
The fish's constant smile moved like a snake underneath the water.

When Snake was Dove's brother-in-law
the reservoir cut across the narrow neck of my dream.

With yellow armpits, a coyote was motioning bad news
tapping on the lake water with the last of his tools.

I floated out over a flooded township, long forgotten.
I wore the lake like a cloak.
Stars swam in and out of my hands.
I floated out over the sunken high school football field.

I floated out over the funeral home
like the effects of the moon on the boloney sandwiches of morticians
when Snake was Dove's brother-in-law.

STRUCK MEAT

Lightning struck the eye
of the family dog
while it drank hail water.

Lightning has sympathy
for no one.

Lightning looked in the window
to see my cousin undress in the mirror,
struck her in the mouth, killed her.

Her boyfriend, touching his lips to juices
of half-cooked meat.

However, my sister
became best friends with lightning.

She married lightning.
Every time a storm approached

sparks flew from her eyebrows and armpits,
red as in the dreams of a person scheduled for the electric chair.

The wagon and mule, Time and Eternity, stop to change places.
　　Their lean and slope-
back shadow, my reservation. The moon moves like infested flour.
　　At the river, bloody
victories meet bloody massacres. They tell each other about their dead.
Grandmothers eat buffalo instead of hamburger. After supper, guitar
　　chords bite through
gravestone. Then the one grandfather interrupts, walking off with his
　　own skull as a lantern into
the polar night. Snowshoe hare cleans the ears of the sleeping and leaves
　　prophetic dreams.
It is quiet. One can hear the hair of the dead grow. The woods, itself,
　　are dressed in frozen
children's clothes. Few of the living disguise themselves as pawned
　　beadwork.

TRYING TO COMMUNICATE WITH A CRACKED
DROID, OUIJA BOARD, MAGIC 8 BALL, AND
COFFEE CANS ABOUT A MESSAGE TRANSCRIBED
ON BIBLE PAPER DIPPED IN THREE-DAY-OLD
COFFEE, THEN BURIED WITH DEMONICALLY
INSPIRED FISH BONES ALONG THE BANKS
OF THE BUFFALO RIVER

You left yourself open.
The soup, so so good.

The weirdo who always wanted
what was not pleasant at all,
ruining it to baby caca.

Tried responding to your message,
looked like you deactivated.

Your face, so just. I wanted to say hi,
wish you a good rest.

Why did you wipe yourself out?
Civilization?

Yes, we saved a few. I hope.
Quality, assurance, fancy for the eternal.

I'm glad I made a difference.
Bueno and God

working through it
like always.

Like a workaholic who has three jobs
at one point.

Lucky, I take a couple of roles.
Four.
Ten.
I want a new droid—screw that smoke signal.

As if it was
the only thing left.

I have words and no computer.
What to do?

As long as I don't see the dead,
I'm fine. Suck it up.

I'm done for the day.
Sucks to be youthful. That was supposed to be you.

NAMESAKE

Your gravesite is a long sidewalk through the Great Plains,
winding through streams,
burning piles of encampments
and archeological digs.

Headstone carved into the shape of your favorite horse.
Its veiny neck stretching out,
looking anxiously westward,
waiting for the spur.

Casket deep as a regiment,
filled with brass buttons,
long beards,
black boots,
bayonets,
Gatling guns,
scouts you got out at front,
crowded around the lid.

This is what archeologists dream about,
but before I had time to, you unraveled
at the shoulders
into a pile of sergeant stripes.

Bones I unfold like a flag,
celebrating you in a broke-ass English,

watching dirt and surprise pour out
from your toothless skull.

While my cranium, a laughing ashtray,
a glued moon missing pieces.

We'll graffiti the name we share
on the forehead of memorials.

HELL'S ACRE

I. THE HEX

Last person doctored on Hell's Acre
was an alcoholic ex-boxer.
Supposedly, later that year, he exhumed all his dead pets
and moved out of state.

I was on Hell's Acre
because I was hexed
by looking into a broken piece of mirror
wrapped in a black silk handkerchief
placed inside my boot.

Ever since, a skeleton followed me,
always trailing so closely behind
like a friend sending me off on my way.

On the west side of the mountains, pine needles were sharper.
I heard a far-off river valley.
I heard panthers summoning rain
to hide their wedding.

The skeleton got scared and held my hand.
The skeleton held my switchblade
on our way down an ancient hog trail.
"Oh, there goes your corpse again," the skeleton lullabied.

That night, fifteenth night of the month,
the moon hesitated to rise after the sun set.

Throughout the valley, all the lost hunting arrows
and knives sang.

I made a campfire.
The skeleton made a grave,
roasted marshmallows over this grave.
We slept at the property gate of a paper company.

I dreamed I was back in Indiahoma
with a case of Coors and all my dead cousins.
I dreamed Indiahoma was a pale star
in the rearview mirror.
I dreamed the eight-headed Mupits carried spiral keys.
I dreamed I was helping Quanah Parker move back into the Star House.
I dreamed the winged snakes came back to the sky.
I dreamed I was dreaming about Ten Bears
and how he drove his knife into his own hand
to prove an obvious point to a bluecoat.
I woke up with my hands bleeding like stigmata.

The skeleton was talking in his sleep
about mason jars filled with blood money buried in dead river mud,
about the governor of the Devil's wardrobe
drinking pop with peanuts floating in it.

I couldn't tell between the humidity and skeleton breath.
The skeleton woke up,
hanging inverted on the fence with the debris.

That damn skeleton flipped me off
when pretending to offer coffee.

After breakfast, at the first willow tree we came to,
I saw four screech owls under it
throwing their eyeballs into the air
and catching them with their eye sockets.
A fox was learning this.

Every now and then, the bones ask,
"When are we not in a dream?
. . . When are we not skeletons?"

III. SECRET ORIGIN OF ESQUELETO

It was Saturday
under the sign of the Siamese.
I placed a half-dollar
on a crescent-moon altar of caliche clay.

The moon taken, chewed up,
then spat into an empty hand
and rubbed in a circular motion to the left.

That's how the wilderness tends to bones.

Every time they prayed for me,
all my worn-out things turned to smoke
and rose to heaven.

Really I was nothing more
than a toothpick from somewhere or another
held in the mouth of an angel
whose name comes from the sound of shivers
it causes
running down people's spines.

A single deerfly cut across
the space of my breath and hovered close
as we both listened
to the excuse of a hundred eternities.

The skeleton says we're together.
We're Siamese twins.
The skeleton thinks we're on an old-style horse raid.
The skeleton put an old horse bone in its mouth
to conjure up a herd.

My Siamese twin is a boring partner
and insists beer be served in cold, beveled mugs.

I need to go back to Indiahoma.
He wants to go to Branson.

We set out on a bicycle with a banana seat.
We listen for stray dogs,
rain clouds popping their collars,
for the Comanche Moon wandering the countryside,
who's not ashamed to laugh
with someone's else blood on its teeth.

So focused on listening,
we pedal out to where
moonlight breaks like a knife blade on the silence.

V. RAID

Lightning out after Beelzebub,
chimera,
medicine.
I had business.

I climbed down a ladder of wolves
to follow unraveled entrails from an old kill.
One can read the future from such.

I took shelter in abandoned blankets
piled high in moonlight
at the border of the floating world.

During a thunderstorm, Zeus and Jesus
licked the rain off each other's hands and arms
like wild animals.
I saw their connection.

The skeleton confided in me and said,
*The two things you do best
are keeping me from dying and telling scary stories* . . .

Then we cut through the Ozarks
like butterflies released by the breath of a vampire.

ACKNOWLEDGMENTS

First, I wish to express my gratitude and appreciation to the National Endowment of the Arts for their generosity and support of my literary endeavors.

Many, many thanks and appreciation to Heid E. Erdrich, editor, and Graywolf Press for the wonderful opportunity to be part of the groundbreaking anthology, *New Poets of Native Nations* (Graywolf Press, 2018).

To the Poetry Foundation and *Poetry* for publishing and sharing my work to the literary world these recent years. They have been a strong supporter.

Finally, to the *New York Times* for featuring my work in their column "New Sentences." The article featured a line from my poem, *Hinterlands*, in their January 25, 2019, Sunday edition.

Poems and portions of this collection have originally appeared or are forthcoming in the following publications and digital sources:

Arkansas International
Before The Usual Time, edited by Darlene Naponse
   (Sudbury, Ontario: Latitude 46 Publishing, 2020)
Dunes Review
Florida Review
Jazz Cigarette
Miracle Monocle
New Poets Of Native Nations, edited by Heid E. Erdrich
   (Minneapolis, MN: Graywolf Press, 2018)
Night Cradle, © Sy Hoahwah (USPOCO Books Chapbook
   Series, 2011)
Pierre Soulages: A Century (Levy Gorvy Gallery, 2019)
Poem-Of-The-Day, Academy of America Poets
Poetry
Recours au Poème

Split, Stuart Hoahwah (Inverted Press Chapbook Series, 2001)
Stoneboat
Tilde: A Literary Journal
World Literature Today